Pop. 1280

Alex Stolis

Copyright© 2021 Alex Stolis
ISBN: 978-93-90601-26-4

First Edition: 2021
Rs. 200/-

Cyberwit.net
HIG 45 Kaushambi Kunj, Kalindipuram
Allahabad - 211011 (U.P.) India
http://www.cyberwit.net
Tel: +(91) 9415091004
E-mail: info@cyberwit.net

Printed at Repro India Limited.

DEDICATION

In 2016 & 2017 I took a road trip through southern and western Minnesota including parts of South Dakota and Iowa looking to make images of the 'real' America. It was miles between towns and sometimes miles between homes. It was not diverse, not thriving, a land locked in the past, the evidence from years of continual migration to urban areas on every Main Street we drove through. In retrospect it appears this is the America of the 'forgotten men and women' who made their voices loud and clear in the 2016 election. This was Trumpland. I wanted to create a project that was documentary style. I decided to write captions for the photos that would tell a story. The project is split into two parts. Part I, On the Run with Dick & Jane, is more of a narrative. Part II, Exiled from Main Street, is more prose style to capture the attitude of a town, an area that is slowly being smothered but at the same time holding on to hope.

The hope is this project can eventually be presented in two separate and different formats. As a gallery type presentation as well as this, a more traditional poetry book.

Camera and gear: I shoot Sony and for this project everything was shot with a Sony a57. The primary lens I used was the Sony 16-50mm f2.8. Some were shot with Sony 18-70mm f3.5-5.6 and Tamron 18-270mm- 3.5-6.3. I like to do minimal of post work and mostly used Snapseed for these photos.

My wife Julie was the inspiration and the literal driving force behind this project. Her creativity and patience made this possible.

Part I

On the Run with Dick & Jane

Kansas would know when the moment was appropriate; know
it as if it were a learned fact. It was a bird with wings, it was dark.
She wanted the lights off. She was never ashamed of her body
and always liked shadows; likes to watch the angled lines of light
hit the sheets and imagines the ocean or the moon or some other
obvious cliché. She wants un-boring, she wants to be an origami
a signature a message in a bottle floating on the crest of a wave.

Paradise was doing 70 mph on the road outside New- Duluth
barreling down the hill to Fond du Lac. Tom was too drunk
to drive, Pat was on the floor of the big Ford boat. Tom rolled
in the bench seat laughing so hard he could barely even talk.
Pat was stoned, head back, hands pounding on the backseat
whooping. Paradise was a kite caught in a tree. Val accused
him of cheating; he couldn't tell her he wanted to die in his
sleep, within reach of all his mistakes.

The day before the earthquake Kansas was drinking red wine,
remembering the first time, knowing how easy it is to confuse
wine for blood, blood for love, love for suffering. She knows
redemption is simple knows what she cannot see, makes a toast;
to the flit of wings and the buzz of leaves in an autumn wind.
She remembers everything, how the world became rock and sky;
quartz and pyrite, how her name, on his lips, became weightless.

It's 2 AM or close enough to last call it doesn't matter. Her name is Felicia or Melissa or doesn't matter. She is the Periodic Table of Elements; argon, oxygen, nitrogen. She's combustible, flammable; one wrong left turn with the right amount of regret. Paradise buys her another drink she rolls a joint tells him Joe Strummer died for their sins. She knows angels are a myth and the way to be saved is to pretend to believe in god. Paradise takes a big hit, holds the smoke in his lungs until it burns raw. She kisses the crucifix around his neck. He has a bullet, give him a gun and he'll shoot the moon.

She imagines herself in a well lit room: white light, white walls, white heat and all the time she'll ever need to make herself over again and again. There is a whisper. There's the cock crow. *You're so pretty when you're unfaithful to me.* She gets dressed. They'll be home any minute. She remembers the first time she rode a bicycle, remembers a rooftop garden, the view of downtown's skyline. She doesn't believe in ghosts or the Father or Son. She believes that once upon a created time there were no heroes or villains; only flat-lands, clouds and dirt.

Paradise is lost. He understands the irony but he's too fucked up
to think it's funny. He had a plan that went to hell, went the way
of all ideas born from desperation: down the swan-neck of a bottle
to be stubbed out on a parquet floor. The lights off Lake Superior
make it look like winter. He can see the frost rough on the window
sill, scratches her initials in sharp angles. Takes off his shoes, crawls
into bed. He wishes to wake to a foreign language and barren trees;
wishes for a crack in the sky large enough to hide himself.

Kansas knows the score. Knows it's a matter of time. Knows time doesn't matter when the score is final. She's convinced of her vulnerability and uncomfortable with her beauty. She takes notes to remember what she has to lose: Christmas, 1963; crying; Dan throwing kisses; sunsets at the lake; crying. She unpacks her books, each one a moment barely alive, each one an opportunity to be left behind or put in the palm of her hand. When she was a child she tried to breathe life into a sparrow. She's ready now; unarmed and invincible.

There are always two women left at last call. They relied on each other to make it through the night unscathed. One wears too much make-up. The other's pretty with the lights down, the perfect amount of drunk. Little Miss Make-Up knows it's a lie but she wants to believe, needs to believe she deserves more than he's willing to give. Ms. Pretty wants another drink, touches his shoulder at the crash of breaking glass as the bartender dumps empties in the trash. That's the sound the world makes when it stops spinning. Paradise tries to catch his breath before the sky rumbles out of view.

She remembers it as if it were some dream song; winter jackets hanging, wet boots in the hall, the smell of fresh cut wood, bitter taste of homemade wine. The trees are more beautiful when they are stripped bare, limbs outstretched to the sky; a lone hawk hunts from the topmost branch. The sun is hidden behind gauze and even the wind can barely breathe. It's the deadest time of year but if you know where to look there is plenty of life. She wants to be in love, just once; utterly, deeply and heroically.

He waits. He waits. He doesn't really want her but settles. She fumbles with his belt buckle. The rain is static electricity. Wet hair in her mouth; a thunder clap. He's heard it all before; the shakes, the bewildered cries of newborn regret [he wishes to wake in a wooden-floored room with a closed blind, a warm bed, her naked body curved into his]. She bites his lip tells him it's time to shut up, time to let the world swallow them whole; time to forget. He kisses her soft, watches the sky turn a deep and failing blue.

Kansas likes to count: the number of steps from kitchen to living room, the number of lines on the wall marking their height. She believes beauty lives in the smallest things: spots of flour on her grandmother's apron, the deep bass of her father's voice bellowing 'Yello! as the screen door slams shut. She remembers mother's plaid skirt, unfiltered cigarettes, remembers the first time she bled. She remembers three-hour long car trips to the Upper Peninsula, pulling over for a carsick brother, a burst of wildflowers; the feeling of being endless, eternal.

Christ, his head was pounding. He would say a prayer but he didn't believe in miracles. He believed his throat was parched, tongue thick; he believed beauty was a ghost he left sleeping in a room at the Budgetel off Hammond. It took a minute for his memory to catch up with him and when it did it bled into dreams and whites and reds. Today feels like burnt orange; birds circle in the cloud-sopped sky. Paradise wants her but never asked for her name, he wants to take back what he said and tell her what he meant. He digs into his pocket for a light, pulls out her number. Yeah. Right. Fuck it.

She knows that love is beauty and beauty is fire and fire is blood. She knows that loss is beauty and beauty is fire and fire is blood stained and painted glass. The day she lost her virginity was cloud less but the sun was gone; the sky honey-dripped and grey. Kansas thought of mortal sins and brimstone and which circle held the most sin. She wondered about paradise and gardens and snakes that talk and a god who walks upright. She called out, to no one: What loves the sky? What loves the hawk circling the field? What loves the field the hawk circles? What loves the girl; her blood afire, her mouth dry?

Paradise makes a list; packs again, and again. It gets dark, then darker. He thinks of scarlet pigeons, thunder; her voice soft and clear. Water's high on the river. There is a shift and center becomes a blur of constant motion. He counts days until he can name them on his fingers. Divides each day into moments: high grass, she's in a slip. Low hung clouds, her shoulder brushing his chin. Thumb hooked in the front pocket of jeans, her eyes pale with morning. It's faith. It's uncertainty. It's time to pack, time to move; time to walk into that bender, break himself in two.

Kansas knows that everyone leaves. Some make it a habit, call it inevitable. Some call it growth or cancer or giving up. She knows about second chances and birds that sit at her window. She says fall is her favorite season. She explained it to him once. Something to do with her father [he was the first to leave]. Something about the way the ground swelled under her feet, how she felt she's part of the earth when she breathed. He tells her he won't leave; makes it a promise. She knows he's not lying. That last time they made love, he cried. She knows, knows uncertainty; knows he'll be gone.

He calls her Pamela. He calls her Barrb [two r's], Julie/Julia/
Juliet. He calls her Valerie [Valerie with the short skirt], Val
[Val with the pierced clit; long before it became de rigueur]
He calls her his favorite bad habit. He calls her inevitability,
the next best chance, the last great hope; he writes directions
on a bar napkin, calls it a story. He waits until all the wheels
fly off because that's what assholes do. This one looked over
board and fanciful; a real sexyhotbuttroubledtype, the right
one/only one left. He was fucked. He just didn't know it yet.

She wants a soundtrack of her life: The Clash for the soccer field; the Stones when he makes her wet; any kind of R&B at all when she doesn't want to pay for her sins. It don't cost much to believe even less to make everything go away. She can feel it in the flicker of a firefly; in every leaf that curls up, crumbles to earth. She wants to hear the sound of him; feel the rhythm of their hips. Wants to feel his rough face on her neck; his sweat mingled with hers. It's too late, she can't start from scratch; can't forget good girls always say no.

He wants to go west or north or south and east, the destination
doesn't matter. It's the doom that counts. It's the running flat-
out, lungs bursting, pockets empty from last shout and the one
before. The Midwest seems like a good place to start, flatlands
and rolling wheat. Upstanding, god-fearing with a perfect view
of the end of the world. Paradise decides to raise the bottom up,
all the way to the roof. If this is the last road, he's going to make
the most from it before the well runs dry.

She can taste mortality. It is metallic and bitter. It is snow on snow and wet and longing. She believes in both existences; the white one where she lives forever in a blade of grass and the black one; where bones and skin are swept into the wind and carried to a misnamed island. She wants to go back to the world; back to front door bangs, small cries. She wants to walk back to simple scars, skinned knees, folded hands and prayers. There. Right there, on the map: a perfect body of water, a broken sky floating to earth like confetti.

He knows it won't be forever. Knows nothing is invincible, lives as if everything cracks. Knows forever's an empty husk; eternity another way to mark time and time is the flutter of a falling leaf; the chill from a vacant touch. He draws a map in the dirt, marks it with initials, marks it with need; wants to mark his way back home. He takes his time in the end because in the end there is nothing. Paradise wants to refurnish himself, wants something, anything solid to hold on to. What he gets is latitudes, longitudes, one painted horse to break; a smooth ride to the next town.

Wherever she happens to be is where she belongs. It's always quiet.
It's the curved neck of an unstrung guitar; the smooth mirrored edge
of a gin bottle left on the kitchen table. Wooden legs stripped bare,
a counter-top edge, stained blood and flaked. Wherever she happens
to be: it could be blonde sand, it could be she's stranded on a newly
paved road waiting for a next good thing. It could make no difference;
it could make her or break away and leave her with nothing. Wherever
she happens to be there is a quickening, a buzz in her blood; the final
note from a long forgotten song.

Paradise sleeps. The sun arcs into a heavy cloud and somewhere is a woman who loves the water, loves the way the wind feels on skin. She watches the blue change to gray to an off white eggshell and wants to paint it; capture it for him and him alone. She notices how cracks in the sky close for lightening. She feels the possibilities that live in a moment, feels the lure of flight. He wants to disappear in a green, green blade of grass, into a clear mist of rain; to the place on the beach where she rests her head.

Part II
Exiled from Main Street

Leaning into the Wind

Her grandmother talked of curses. Passed down generations
They're a noose and a lifeline. Handmade. A pale band on her
Ring finger. Sometimes she unfolds herself. He doesn't notice
Anymore. It doesn't really matter. This is not where it started
To fall apart. That was long ago. Before any curse was burned
Into their DNA. Before the drought and the famine long before
The ground could no longer be turned.

In the beginning heaven was still and dark

In the beginning the sky was a kaleidoscope of ash and smoke.
On the seventh day God rested from all his work. On the eighth
There was no sound at all. The silence was turquoise. Smooth
And shiny it covered the earth. A thin sheet of glass. Right now
It's cold. The sun seems too far away and we have been awake
For hours. This world has its own sins to confess its own truths
To bury. Let's keep ours in the hollow of stillness, in the deepest
Red of this darkness that sticks to everything.

Do you remember how Jesus told fables to the apostles

Did they ever wonder when he turned water into wine
Or raised the dead if God had more surprises. Did they
Know the sun isn't hot. Stars are not light. Grass seems
To bend but is rigid. She tells a story about her mother.
There's silence. Wind. Windows bang open/shut. Music
Stops. There's only one more moon to shoot. She dreams
Of angel-ghosts, secret denouements; remembers the last
Time he kissed her, open-mouthed, expectant. She's paled
And flush. God is not finished with us.

Skateaway

She is nowhere. She's exactly where she's supposed to be.
She was born for now. She lets him undress her. Closes her
Eyes. Can smell the grass. Raising her arms the sun swallows
Her whole. They are made from time, air, words, fragments
Of sound. There's nothing between them. Space measured
In sentences, paragraphs, lines that break over and through
The sky. He becomes nameless. She watches as the skeleton
Trees bend toward heaven, wraps herself around the world.

Stolen Car

I send my grief away. I want change. Want it good.
The back and forth of guilt, the black and white of
Yearning. Wish we could go there: out in the open
Unafraid and insatiable. I want change. Want it bad.
Johnny Cash died the day after my father's birthday
Fall leaves were bandaged and blue. The earth mud
-Scarred and green. All we ever had to do was reach
Out to touch the end of the world, jagged and dull.

I used to believe upon death we wandered the earth

Searching for signs of ourselves, the self we thought we were
Not the barely recognizable us dressed up/cleaned up in a suit
Or dress never worn when we were alive. I supposed there was
A sun we could no longer feel on our face, a brilliant sterile glow
Devoid of warmth. We would realize our houses were made of
Boxes; tin, steel, cardboard, pine, filled half empty from wishes
Born in yesterday's dying light. Imagined we'd feel the dirt under
Our bare feet. We'd ramble from room to room from box to box
Hollow-boned and silent. Ready to become imagined.

Adam Raised a Cain

The land celebrates men of war. The land changes from green
To sickly red. I'm a fistful of earth. I am small. In a small world
Long gone I'm a spent match on the floor, an un-tuned guitar.
We're a bored, disinterested house. We're stranded and burnt
Out; we're straw men blinded by primary color. There's warmth
In the corners we've lived. The days we can rest away are brittle
Sharpened bone. The sky's empty, a hollow promise. Our languid
Prayers are a shuffle and mumble. We mend our ways too late.

Never isn't as long as we think

We are impermanence, filaments of light. We are not straight
Lines drawn from Point A to Forever highlighted in transparent
Blue. We spin ourselves tales. Of beginnings, of firsts. First kiss
First touch. First fuck. We mythologize impatience, fumble with
Buttons, snaps, belts unbuckled and hair unpinned. We become
A sonic boom rattling windows and shaking walls as if never can
Be measured by decibels. Not how long we can hold our breath.

One day without warning we discover we have no choice

No direction. We've become a recurring dream ramrodding
Our way through lost hours. We spend weekends over dim
Light, cigarette smoke, undressing each other while reading
Psalms to tamp down passion, suffocate lust. We try to find
Divine intervention between whispers, in the soft orbit of our
Little death. Together, we'll carry the ashes of sin to the river
Douse ourselves under the moon. Until then let's complicate
The obvious and sanctify the banal. Transform each other into
A fierce necessity. Be reborn as ghosts between cloud and sky.

God lives in a distant sky

Christ was a fisherman. He knew the echo of the sea the roiling
Thunder of waves. Water can't hold you tight in its fist like land,
Can't carry it in pockets. It doesn't become imbedded under our
Nails, caked in our skin. The ground is firm, it's tangible. Not sky
Or air or heaven. There's no moon to hang, no stars to shoot. It's
Forever, it's a past present future tense we speak. Our language
Our life histories built and buried in wood and iron, fire and faith.
We're apostles of the soil. This's all there is. This's it. The one law.

We are handcuffed to the bottom of the world

We dream of cornfields study the patterns in frost. We love
A just lit match. It reminds us of an April sun, lifts the dull out
From our hearts. This air is breakable, a pale skin that covers
Our world and sky. You say there're some attachments worth
The suffering. There's no distance between us, space defined
By words, numbers, color. Crows congregate on a bare branch,
Thin outline on a flat horizon. I'm so sorry. I can't shake off this
Chill. Can't zen us out of this mess. I'm frozen, inadequate, my
Limbs made of stone. This is the place where goodbye belongs.

Badlands

We make our own religion because God is a shifty character
Seemingly bent on our demise. No longer able to cover our
Disappointment with faith, we mumble prayers over hollow
Demigods. We argue about unwritten commandments want
To build walls separate ourselves from what is real and what
We hope for. She rests her hand on your forearm says today
Is your lucky day, to trust the Ouija the tarot the myths you
Created. *Let's light candles, see our future in the electric red
And blue flicker.* You feel her lips graze yours, feel the flutter
Of something lost. That's the moment you believe.

Dylan never really lived here

It's a lonesome street in a gone town. It's where she lost
Her voice. I'm an uncooperative witness a fly amber-ed
In the ointment. Once upon a time we called each other
Best friends, last lovers. Pretended we were descended
From heroes were going to change our names. Her mom
Made all her dresses, *handmade hand-me-downs*. When
We kissed it wasn't magical, charmed. We never believed
In fairytale endings, origin myths or luck. We live our lives
Down the middle of gravity. Where all the hungry people
Have pale skin and assassin's eyes.

There is no comfort anywhere for anyone who dreads to go home

Torment no longer wounds us we're on the cusp of freedom
Looking backwards. Anchoring ourselves to the world but too
Small to reverse the spin we hold tight to each other. White
Smoke is rising, the river runs dry. A Red Tailed hawk perched
On a branch clocks a rabbit skittering through the overgrown
Lot. Your hand slips into my back pocket further penance may
Be required so you kiss me full on the mouth. He's off, silence
Cuts an unforgiving line through this wet summer day. I watch
The sun shrug off the horizon, wrap my arms around you.
Run Rabbit. Run.

One day we hope to be real enough

To rebuild ourselves from scratch. To remember the crash of sea
As it was being parted. You slip one hand over her heart, arson on
Your mind. The fields are scarred with muddy furrows. There's no
Use in pretending to care about anything. Love is a stone burrowed
Deep in the ground, her kiss ink-stained and sweet. One day you'll
Be solid and forever. Until then hold her close. Feel the blood red
Unravel from dusk, see the moon thread its way through the stars.

Dream Song 44

It was the first day of spring; like any other day but flatter;
A tight-chested-wait-for-the-shoe-to-drop day. We tried to
Be good, tried to placate the part time gods. Parked cars
Heat up on Main Street. She's newly minted in her halter
Top, sling backs and black tights; that buzz should be over
By now. I watch the sun fight shadows on the downtown
Skyline; can't keep anything, can't imagine words anymore
Without you in them. You play piano: soft, low; a prayer,
A processional song for saints and the forgotten. Me, I have
To say everything twice; make sure I believe.

She said we become imaginary too soon

She doesn't remember being that girl, someone else remembered
Her that way. Says it feels like a gift to have a piece of her returned.
I imagine that girl, barefoot, on a mission. Picking a flower for each
Sunfish her father caught. A celebration of fish, of light, water, dark
With rust. And now, here we are, sins buried in the soft pop and click
Of raindrops. Windows rolled down, Johnny Cash on the radio,
Open Roads and clean skies; endless possibilities, endless.

We want to believe our minds will keep us safe

But they won't. I tell her that sometimes I practice
Dying; fully-winged, eyes closed, waiting for a crash
Of wind. Someone passes the basket. We take what
We need and leave the rest. We're ready to preamble.
I catch her glance. Imagine we're lolling on a beach
In Kerouac's Mexico. She knows we're already there,
Whiskey's in a row, a tapestry of sand and every word
Ever uttered waiting for high tide to wash us away.

Untitled reading a letter

It's easier to love by subscription; lines are straight in auto-response,
Nothing to read between or beyond. There is nothing deeper; it is face
Value with time stamp attached. The system is simple, fail-safe and
Sound proof. I'm the perfect song surrounded by a circle of black birds;
Can't even guess what you may be doing at this moment. Are your hands
Cupped around morning coffee, bare feet on hardwood floors? I can no
Longer imagine the mundane; can't envision a future beyond air, mist
And the loud bang of nothing.

Promised Land

I remember what we never did: catching the last rites
Of summer like the Zapruder film, your fingers looped
'Round my belt. It was a clean getaway, we were home
Free and unaware.

www.ingramcontent.com/pod-product-compliance
Lightning Source LLC
LaVergne TN
LVHW052318210726
843527LV00028B/424